The Alpha Male Blueprint
Discover What Women Really Want and Make Them Chase You With Dating Secrets to Become a Charming, Confident, Powerful, and Legendary Alpha Man in No Time.
Eric Holt

Copyright © 2023 by Eric Holt

All rights reserved.

It is not legal to reproduce, duplicate, or transmit any part of this document in either electronic means or in printed format. Recording of this publication is strictly prohibited and any storage of this document is not allowed unless with written permission from the publisher except for the use of brief quotations in a book review.

ISBN: 9781835123256

Contents

Introduction	V
1. Unleashing Your Inner Alpha	1
What Is An Alpha Male?	
Understanding The Traits Of An Alpha Male	
Embracing The Alpha Mindset	
2. Mastering The Art Of Confidence	16
Developing Unshakable Confidence	
Enhancing Your Social Skills	
3. What Women Want	22
Decoding Female Psychology	
Building Emotional Connection	
Free Goodwill	33
4. Becoming Irresistible	35
The Alpha Man's Guide To Flirting	
Seduction Techniques That Drive Women Wild	
5. Dating Strategies For Alpha Men	49
Navigating The Dating Scene With Confidence	
The Art Of Making A Powerful First Impression	
6. Balancing Inner And Outer Strength	58
What Exactly Is Self-Care, And Why Do Men Need It?	
Nurturing The Body, Mind, And Soul	

Managing Stress And Overcoming Burnout

Conclusion 67

Introduction

You'll know how to approach a female once you learn how to make them chase you. Gaining a girl's attention and, eventually, her heart depends entirely on the pursuit.

Once you figure out how to get her, you'll see that winning her love and affection is easy. There is a reason why women are consistently seen as complex people. However, mastering the art of making women chase you requires a deeper understanding of women and their motivations.

The difficult part is to get through her defenses so she feels at ease with you and is willing to chase you.

Even if males have excellent intentions, girls often find it difficult to trust and open up to them. She will be interested in you if you can pique her desire, which is what the chase is about.

It's a battle to win them over, so the chase is exciting for both men and women. Desire separates her from repeatedly telling you she is "busy" anytime you want to hang out and into a persistent inquiry about your availability.

This is another reason there are so many rules about not calling her the next day or being too clingy too soon. You'll eventually see how ridiculous these restrictions are, yet they also have a purpose.

Uncomfortably, until you prove to her that you're worth the chase, passion can be difficult to control. You can start to impress and pique her interest if you can distinguish yourself from the other males who showed up earlier.

Men typically judge a woman's attractiveness based on her appearance and make this determination within the first few minutes of their first encounters. They might initially be infatuated with her and subsequently decide that she isn't worth it or become distracted by someone else, though this can change. How you treated her when you first started talking to her greatly impacts your relationship with her. Making a girl fall in love with you is not that difficult, and we ensure you are at the top of your game. The ones that succeed in getting the girl are the ones who never pursue it. Men who are hard to get and don't chase women are also popular with women.

So, here are some suggestions to help you become an alpha male and win her heart. We devised ten chapters to make the ladies swoon and follow us!

1
Unleashing Your Inner Alpha

Do you ever notice guys who seem to have everything going for them? They are in excellent form, have the most alluring, successful companions, and their work lives are constantly humming.

It could be tempting to think they've discovered a genie who can fulfill their wishes, but our society sees men who act that way as alpha males.

You may still have a negative impression of "alpha males" from high school or college who are aggressive, loud, and fierce. Guys like them are merely annoying, despite thinking they represent "alpha status" worldwide.

Being a real alpha male is more about how you run your life than how others see and treat you. You can do anything once you understand that being an alpha male is about authority over your destiny.

Let's examine the characteristics and routines of really successful alpha males and discuss how you can make the decision that will transform your life.

What Is An Alpha Male?

The belief that alphas dominate within a social hierarchy is the foundation for the general ideas of "alphas" and "betas" in males.

Although even the renowned wolf research creator that gave rise to the term "alpha" has subsequently revised his mind, this may be true in animals. Men who erroneously portray themselves as combative alphas are typically bullies who won't give in.

The first thing to realize is that alpha status has nothing to do with conflict or confrontation; it comes from being in control of your own life.

A beta male, for instance, travels where the wind takes him. He goes to work at a job he doesn't enjoy because it keeps food on the table and pays the rent.

He faithfully attends to his 401(k) and conscientiously marries a lady he obediently loves but lacks passion for, planning to retire one day when he is elderly, and life has passed him by.

Alphas see every day as a chance to improve their lives, their place in the world, and the lives of others around them. He's constantly seeking new ways to succeed, whether discovering side hustles that could lead to long-term entrepreneurship or finding a fulfilling job. The alpha males look out for themselves, plan for the future, and live each day to the fullest.

In other words, alphas take control of their lives rather than trying to escape them through vice and leisure.

Understanding The Traits Of An Alpha Male

Most alpha males are often perceived as self-confident, powerful, successful people with leadership traits. Others around them appreciate them and are at ease taking the initiative and making decisions. But what precise indications might you look for in an alpha male?

Whether looking for clues that an alpha male likes you, trying to spot one in your own life, or wanting to know more about this idea, read on to understand the nine real indicators of successful alpha males.

Alphas Speak And Persuade With Dignity And Respect

Alphas are often considered self-confident and assertive, but they can be problematic if these traits are not applied with decency and consideration.

Empathy and the capacity to hear and comprehend the viewpoints of others are necessary for persuasive behavior and effective communication. The ability to do this is a sign of an alpha man's capacity to set aside his ego and take into account the wants and desires of others. This exhibits a degree of maturity and self-awareness necessary for effective leadership.

Additionally, alphas who treat others respectfully when communicating and persuading others are more likely to forge enduring bonds and foster a welcoming environment. They can persuade others without force or deceit, and their communication style is probably longer-lasting and more successful. This holds for both verbal and nonverbal cues. Alpha male body language is open, confident, and courteous, and there is a lot of eye contact.

Overall, demonstrating leadership, integrity, and the capacity to forge strong bonds through respectful communication and persuasion indicates an alpha male. These traits are necessary for any effective leader, and they play a significant role in what defines an alpha male as such.

Alphas Are Aware Of Their Flaws

Alphas regard failure and perceived flaws as opportunities to grow rather than threats to their status or identity. Since they understand that taking chances and trying new things is the best way to develop and succeed, they are willing to do so even if there is a potential for failure.

A true alpha male can also accept his frailties and faults as essential to his identity. He doesn't try to hide or downplay his flaws; instead, he seeks to strengthen them and make the most of them.

Someone with alpha male energy can show tenacity and resolve without fearing failure or perceived shortcomings.

Alphas Are Self-Confident

Alpha males have faith in their capacity to pave their way. Trusting your instincts is paying attention to and acting on your inner guidance despite opposition from others or attempts to convince you otherwise. It necessitates self-confidence, the capacity to believe in yourself, and the capacity for self-reliance.

Even in doubt, an alpha male who follows his instincts can act swiftly and decisively. He trusts his skills and knows his gut will guide him on the right path.

An alpha man must, however, be conscious of the limitations of relying exclusively on his instincts. Before making a choice, gathering information and considering additional considerations is crucial. An alpha male who trusts his instincts while still taking the time to assess the circumstance carefully can make wise and calculated decisions.

Overall, the capacity to follow your intuition is a true hallmark of an alpha male because it exhibits confidence, self-awareness, and the capacity for quick and deliberate action.

Alphas Look For Real Ties

You cherish genuine ties with others as an alpha male. You're not interested in partnerships or conversations solely to meet your wants. Instead, you care about supporting others and being there for them when they require advice or support.

Naturally, this does not imply that you can always assist them. You could have times when your needs come first, whether putting them first in a relationship or taking care of your physical and emotional needs. However, you generally try to support others and forge deep bonds. You also experience great fulfillment and satisfaction from interacting with others as you forge these connections.

Alphas Aim For Improvement And Mastery

Alpha males constantly strive to improve and master their craft. As alpha males, they recognize that success in all facets of life requires continuous self-improvement. They also recognize that life is an ever-evolving journey. This desire for personal development and mastery takes many forms, including ongoing learning, goal-setting, achievement, measured risks, and continuous self-improvement.

Alphas often want to surround themselves with people who can help them develop as individuals since they constantly try to improve themselves. They are aware that they cannot always rely on their ability to succeed in life; rather, they must seek the advice and help of others. They constantly look for mentors who can help them on their road to success.

Alphas are aware of the necessity to create goals and take decisive actions to achieve those goals to develop themselves continuously. They establish difficult but reachable goals based on their special skills and shortcomings. They then take action to achieve these goals by formulating a detailed action plan that specifies benchmarks and due dates for completing each component of the goal.

Alpha males constantly strive to improve and master their craft.

Alphas Battle Their Demons

Contrary to popular assumption, being an alpha man entails more than having superior physical attributes and leading other men. It also entails facing your inner demons and learning how to cope healthily.

Although many people view alphas as the definition of masculinity, they have a more vulnerable side that is often overlooked. Being an alpha entails recognizing those emotions of self-doubt and dread and developing good coping mechanisms. This can be accomplished through psychotherapy, support groups, or other forms of therapy.

Using mindfulness practices like deep breathing and meditation is a good approach for alphas to conquer their inner demons. Alphas can learn to control their emotions better, forge relationships with others, and enhance their general wellbeing by often practicing these skills.

Alpha Males Are Polite

Because they are self-confident and affable, true alphas have little trouble attracting women. Because he has the power to boost their self-esteem, the alpha man is someone to whom women are drawn. But being flamboyant or domineering isn't the only way people will be drawn to an alpha.

Instead, he lets his genuine qualities as a gentleman and a man of integrity speak for themselves. Women drawn to this type of love partner value that he is manly without being overbearing. He is skilled at playing the role of the natural leader and "macho guy," but he does so in a way that makes his followers respect and admire him rather than fear or dislike him.

Alphas Are "Change It Or Accept It"

It has long been recognized that alpha males have a "change it or accept it" mentality regarding their choices and objectives. The ability to immediately adapt to any changes and the willingness to meet them head-on and maintain their commitment to the course set before them are characteristics of this attitude. One of the most significant characteristics of an alpha male's mentality is that same thinking, and anyone who wants to take on the world can master it.

This mentality may be seen in how alpha guys interact with others and approach situations and challenges. They often have an authoritative and forthright demeanor and don't hesitate to express their opinions.

Alpha Males Are Assertive And Take Care Of Themselves

Even though it is awkward or unpopular, an alpha man won't hesitate to speak up when he sees something that has to be expressed or done. He knows that maintaining his physical and mental health is crucial to his capacity to lead and succeed.

He doesn't mind deviating from the norm, openly opposing others, or expressing his ideas on any topic. However, he is also willing to change his position and admit when he is mistaken, demonstrating that he values honesty and adaptability above all else.

Embracing The Alpha Mindset

Having an Alpha Male Mindset is essential for success with women. Dominance and confidence, two characteristics often associated with alpha males, are attractive to women. Here are some pointers for cultivating an alpha male mindset:

Stop Being Afraid

This does not imply that you shouldn't feel fear; it's impossible. Alphas still experience fear but purposefully carry out their intended course of action.

The distinguishing characteristic of an alpha male is understanding the risks and having the self-confidence to deal with any potential drawbacks of choice.

Prevent Pointless Conflict

Whether you're about to argue with your girlfriend or someone rams into you at the bar, a man with alpha male features realizes that fighting isn't helpful.

Always try to understand why someone could be upset or furious with you. This does not imply that you must submit to their demands, but it highlights the difficulty of reflection and its importance in all facets of your life. Repeat it often!

Look After Yourself

Salads, sleep, cleanliness, and flossing are not sexy, but we do them because they keep us healthy.

To become an alpha, in addition to performing CrossFit a few times per week, you must manage your stress and mental health.

His hormones and feelings still rule a man who has complete control over everything but his anger, and he will never be able to be an alpha.

Don't Ever Think You're Good At Sex

With a few moves, moderate stamina, and the unreliable compliments of a few sexual partners, many men get by in life.

But since sex is a team sport, your teammate will find a new partner if unsatisfied. Even worse, your performance will suffer if you are self-conscious about your sexual prowess.

Learning a few new techniques, getting help with premature ejaculation or erectile dysfunction, and improving your sexual skills are all effective ways to increase your power, which will increase your confidence.

Avoid Looking For Numbness

Many people are content to crack open a few drinks and binge-watch television when they should follow their interests, such as producing, starting a business, or chiseling fat into rock-hard abs.

Whatever your vice may be—porn, video games, alcohol, or weed—it's undoubtedly shortening your life and your attention span.

Even when we just want to relax, the traits of an alpha guy push us toward discomfort and growth.

Additionally, it feels much better to relax on the couch with a nice drink when we've worked hard to earn it by improving ourselves.

Discover Joy Through Purpose

What are you doing with your life if you don't have a purpose? What are you working for if you merely go to work to get the money you spend on vices and leisure activities?

Are you happy to perform like a machine at work in exchange for the "privilege" of using your free time to pursue disconnectivity? Find your mission and vigorously pursue it until you can turn it into a profession.

Give Your Time Rather Than Money (Volunteer)

Alphas work to improve society, beginning with their local area. Discover your neighborhood's breadline or homeless shelter and learn how you can help.

And while giving money is wonderful and noble, giving your time is much better. Since time is a limited resource, using it to serve others develops character. Join social clubs that engage in volunteer work, coach, teach guitar to impoverished children in your neighborhood, work on a community garden, go grocery shopping for your elderly neighbors, etc.

Do everything you can to make a difference for those around you.

Stop Awaiting Rescue From Others

Everyone who has achieved success in life has had help in some way; alpha males are no different. Nobody has ever achieved success in life by working alone.

But this is not the same as hoping for success from someone else. You'll always be a beta male if you're standing about waiting for people to give you money.

This is still true when you patiently wait to "get rewarded" at work with a raise or promotion. Never wait for someone else to permit you to better your life if you want to advance in your job.

Don't Depend On Others To Make You Happy

Suppose your partner's happiness or your kids' approval of you only makes you happy. In that case, you'll probably behave badly, which includes failing to correct your children and not standing up to your relationship.

Stop sacrificing your joy as an expense to appease others in the near term. Nobody appreciates a pushover. The things you love and your life goals should bring you happiness. Don't ask others for their blessing to be happy.

Be Ready For A Fight (But Don't Go Looking For One)

You'll have difficulty resisting conflict if you don't feel confident that you can defend yourself in a fight.

It's more important to be able to defend yourself if someone were to come after you than to be able to street fight like Jackie Chan.

Higher confidence levels are attained when you know you can face anyone trying to intimidate you.

Follow Your Dreams Embarrass-Free

Want to compose the follow-up to "Hamilton" but are worried that your friends will mock you for it? Make new friends.

Contrary to what others may think, following your happiness is preferable to limiting it to what may win their approval.

We're not advising you to get a tattoo of "dance like nobody's watching" on your ankle, but that's okay. Instead, it shouldn't matter if someone is watching you or you're doing something you love.

Do Not Fear Resting

Since you're used to beer, Netflix binges, and the status quo, these adjustments may already sound taxing, and they will be.

But that's okay because it's equally necessary to unwind and replenish as it is to push yourself hard.

Get a massage (or use a massager), watch your sleep hygiene, and learn when to say "no" to taking on extra responsibility.

Take Care Of Yourself

Men don't necessarily need to shave with a straight razor in a mountain stream with a bear howling in the distance as part of their self-care routine. Using skincare, sexual health, and hair care products is acceptable.

Self-mastery, which involves self-care practices, leads to confidence. Get rid of the heteronormative gender biases, and understand the benefits of small self-care.

Keep Your Promises

Whether or not you follow your commitments is one of the key things people remember about you, especially for your children.

Make only those commitments you can fully keep since nothing is more upsetting than being betrayed or disappointed by someone you love and trust.

Everyone you encounter will remember you for being a man of your word if you try to be one.

Establish Your Values And Uphold Them

We're not advocating that you pen a classic on your values, but you should begin by outlining them yourself.

Establish your beliefs and what is essential to you, and then use them to establish a foundation for your decisions.

Develop Your Voice

Everyone seems to believe their opinion must be heard, even if it is incorrect, especially with social media.

While arguing online is easy, sticking up for what is right in person is completely different.

Alphas develop the confidence to speak up in uncomfortable circumstances, regardless of the location. See how much your perspective of yourself changes when you stand up for yourself and those around you.

Embrace The Discomfort

An alpha male is aware that pain leads to progress, whether you're trying to achieve your ideal body, starting a business, or having relationship issues.

Realizing this is not enough; you must also learn to crave the discomfort that comes with growing as a person.

We have innate desires for calories, sexual partners, and leisure and want to attain those things as quickly as possible. Learn to appreciate the pain of growth; it's better than the anguish of regret since achievement, education, and muscle growth all come from the soil of pain.

Be Assertive

The status quo has never resulted in anything positive. You're only distancing yourself if you're worried about upsetting your partner, employer, or the most important people in your company.

Living your life by other people's standards isn't the best way to go, as you only have one life to live. Do not mistake this as a license to be obnoxious or disrespectful; instead, be firm about what you want, even if it means offending someone.

If your partner or friends are bothered by your getting better, they aren't on your side.

Don't Be A "Nice" Guy

Alpha males are helpful and kind to others because they genuinely care about them. Betas or "nice guys" only act kind when they want something in return or because they fear being treated unfairly by others.

Be Self-Reliant

Alphas draw strength from within, even in the face of adversity. Recognize that even if everything goes wrong, you can still use your brain and willpower to improve your life.

If you want to know if you're on the right track, don't ask other people; that's what beta men would do. Instead, come to your conclusion.

Stop Asking Yourself, "How Do I Become An Alpha Male."

You presumably had an idea of what being "alpha" meant before you started reading this book, and it was probably based on external cues rather than innate confidence.

Recognize that being the alpha means setting your course and controlling your destiny.

2
Mastering The Art Of Confidence

What sort of confidence attracts women to you? Many dating experts advise you to have the confidence to succeed with women.

A confident man will show he is in control and aware of his values, goals, and dissatisfactions.

Others will not readily sway a man who has self-confidence. They are determined leaders and have a strong sense of self-awareness. These all suggest that he is strong and trustworthy.

Men who have a strong sense of self-confidence are irresistible to women. Because of this, it is widely recommended that you project confidence to draw women to you.

Every man is aware of the need to possess confidence, but how? You should be aware that self-confidence is a collection of beliefs if you want to develop strong self-confidence with women. Learn more about boosting your self-confidence.

What sort of confidence are the dating experts talking about, then? Many men struggle to understand how to be the kind of confident person that naturally attracts women.

Therefore, although they know the need for confidence, they are unsure how to convey it. I break down the self-confidence below so you may learn what kind of confidence naturally draws women. Continue reading.

Developing Unshakable Confidence

Confidence doesn't just appear one day. You must put in the effort every day if you want to appeal to ladies. Confidence is a mindset.

Let's look at four things you may do to boost your self-confidence and attract the woman of your dreams.

Look After Your Body

Let's face it; women adore a man who takes care of his body. One of the best methods to increase self-confidence is through this. When you feel wonderful about yourself and your appearance, the other sex may find you alluring. More significantly, exercise promotes mental health.

The most physically active, fittest, and strongest men reported lower stress levels than those with lower scores in these areas. They performed better on assessments of their "mental resources" as measured by their vigor, aptitude, and confidence in their daily tasks.

I'm not saying you have to appear like Hercules, but first impressions are influenced by physical appeal. Pay attention to how you look in a way that boosts your self-confidence. Hit a gym, start lifting weights, and watch as your confidence soars once you attract the attention of the women you've been looking for.

Be Presentable

You only get one chance to leave a lasting impression. Have you ever considered the impression other women could get from how you dress? What you put on says a lot about your personality and what is important to you. Women are wise to this sort of thing.

Would you dress in worn-out jeans and a wrinkled shirt to impress a woman at a bar? No. You'd put on attire for success! It's not necessary to go all out to appear good. Choose clothing that passes the message you want to communicate to ladies and develop a look that reflects who you are.

This is a fantastic method to boost your self-confidence and feel at ease in your skin.

Practice Your Nonverbal And Verbal Communication Skills

Communication is vital when it comes to dating and attracting a woman. Many men get bogged down in this situation. If you don't feel confident, it will be obvious in your body language.

Men who are shy and anxious sometimes glance down, cross their arms, and hunch their shoulders to make themselves look smaller. This behavior does not appeal to women and conveys, "I'm closed off and don't want to talk to you."

MASTERING THE ART OF CONFIDENCE

Your posture has an impact on how you feel. Practice holding your head high while standing tall with your shoulders back. Simply changing your posture will make you feel more confident right away.

Maintain constant eye contact and pay attention to what a woman is saying when you are speaking to her. Don't try dominating the discussion; ask her about herself. Praise her for her brains or sense of humor. The emphasis is on being sincere and true.

From a mile away, a lady can smell cheese. She will, however, compliment you if she thinks you're being serious.

Push Your Comfort Zone To The Limit

A man's confidence might be destroyed if he ventures outside his comfort zone and is rejected by a woman. He might therefore continue to avoid new circumstances or settings that make him feel uneasy among women.

But if you just venture outside your comfort zone, you'll never succeed in luring the woman of your dreams. You must approach attractive ladies, start conversations, and learn to accept rejection. It all comes down to daily incremental steps. You can only improve if you're prepared to experience discomfort and awkwardness when you try anything new.

You don't need to go overboard or do anything so uncomfortable that you get a panic attack. Start easy. When you see a girl in the store, smile, hold the door open for her, or say something nice about her outfit. Who cares if she ignores you or if she doesn't? You've taken a step toward meeting a woman who will.

Enhancing Your Social Skills

You will benefit from learning to develop your social skills in almost every area of your life. But really, where else can you practice social skills more than with women? It's a killer way to do it, but enhancing your social skills with women will also enhance your social skills in every other area of life. It will inspire you much if nothing else. Read on to learn how to improve your social skills with women and other facets of life.

Set A Goal For It

You must first set this as a goal if you want to learn how to become more social with women. You must make up your mind to do it. This implies that you must acquire the necessary knowledge, find time to exercise your abilities and resolve to carry it through. You won't automatically accomplish it by reading this book. You will only receive the necessary materials to begin developing your social skills. It is up to you to use the tools.

Go Outside More

You need to start going out more often, or at the very least, spend the time you do go out more wisely if you want to learn how to enhance your social skills with women. You need to start chit-chatting with women when you go out. Decide how many ladies you want to talk to in one night and set reasonable goals for yourself. This will allow you to hone your social skills while also helping you become more at ease while speaking to women, possibly the most crucial social skill you can have when raising your game's difficulty.

Talk To Women Wherever You Go

But it's not only about nightclubs and bars. We genuinely think a man with well-developed social skills can talk to ladies everywhere, even on the bus, at a coffee shop, and while merely strolling down the street. Develop your social abilities in situations where others wouldn't typically interact. It also enables you to develop new social skills you didn't even know you possessed. This is one of the best methods to feel more at ease speaking to ladies.

No Pain, No Gain

If you exercise, you know that if you aren't pushing yourself when lifting, your body won't change. Similarly, this is true for social skills. You won't develop the social skills you want to, which will make you very effective in almost any circumstance if you don't push yourself past your comfort zone. Remember that one of your goals in developing your social skills is to reduce some of the awkwardness you may feel around others.

3
What Women Want

What women want in a relationship is a subject that has baffled men for generations.

Men sometimes have no idea how to respond to questions like this because of gender disparities. We discuss understanding what women want in a relationship, especially from their male partners. Every woman has a mystery, and men must understand it to satisfy them.

Even the smartest men are challenged by the intricacies of women. Even the most intelligent guys are still perplexed by what women desire in a relationship.

Men's relationships with women are largely determined by their energy, motivation, happiness, self-confidence, money, social standing, and life expectancy. In a heterosexual relationship, a man's behavior influences a woman's happiness.

The simple truth is that everything hinges on how a man perceives a woman's feelings and how he reacts to them. There is no such thing as right or wrong or a list of dos and don'ts. It has to do with a man's want to understand his lady.

Decoding Female Psychology

Men often have a hard time understanding women. For you, that issue is resolved today. This will help you join the select group of men aware of these eight secrets of female psychology.

Knowing the reasons behind your love interest's actions and how to react makes dating much easier. So, let's get started.

Women Aren't Just Interested In Your Appearance

Biology underlies attraction. It primarily depends on one's capacity to provide healthy children for other children. For this reason, men prefer young women with wide hips, large breasts, and a narrow waist. It explains why women consider factors other than a man's attractiveness.

Women traditionally needed a strong, manly guy to care for them and their families. Even while it's less crucial today, women are wired to focus more on a man's personality than his appearance.

Women care about your appearance, but largely for the impression it gives them of you. Being tall and powerful indicates that you can take care of her. She'll presume you can't care for yourself if you're not well dressed and groomed.

Some younger females seek out attractive men to receive the affirmation of dating a pretty boy; however, once she develops into a self-confidence, sophisticated lady, that becomes significantly less significant.

Although Few Women Will Admit It, Most Women Are Open To Casual Sex

Both men and women enjoy sex. They have to be more selective about who they sleep with, which is the difference. If they pick the wrong companion, the consequences will be even more severe.

One of these repercussions is having a negative reputation. It could be seriously harmful if it becomes known that she is "easy." Women know that excellent men won't want to have a family with someone who rides a "village bicycle." They, therefore, make every effort to escape this label.

Women develop lust. Women may want casual sex. However, they need to keep it under wraps.

Invite a woman to your home after her friends have left if you want to try to have a brief fling. Better yet, find a good excuse to go there so she may claim to her friends that "it just happened" and "one thing led to another." Or you two might claim nothing happened.

Thanks to dating apps, organizing a covert one-night stand is now easier than ever. We now live in a "hook-up culture" as a result. Some teenage girls have abstained from it. Even still, the majority who have won't confess it.

Women Desire Your Leadership

Additionally, attraction is strongly influenced by sexual polarity. More manly males attract females.

Women want you to take the initiative since you are a strong leader with many masculine qualities. They also expect you to initiate contact, pick the venue for the date, choose when to kiss them, etc.

A man who asserts himself allows his girlfriend to unwind and celebrate her femininity. Only then will she start to get excited.

Women React To Emotions Rather Than Reason

Logic is the focal point of masculine force. Emotion is the focal point of feminine energy. Because of this, girls choose the exciting guy over the boring one who would make a great boyfriend on paper.

Your best chance of winning a woman's heart is to play on her feelings. Why do you suppose women like to date unstable "bad boys"? These people are illogical, yet they offer a roller-coaster of highs and lows in terms of emotions.

Women Will Always Prioritize Their Safety

You will typically be larger and more powerful than the woman you are pursuing. Be mindful of how intimidating this is.

Until you prove otherwise, most women will view you as a scary creep. Because of this, it could take them some time to get used to you.

You can demonstrate that you're not a creep by displaying good social skills. Smile. Maintain friendly eye contact. Analyze her nonverbal cues. Respond if she shows signs of discomfort, respond.

Putting on for your female friends is also beneficial. Bring them with you to the celebration. Post images of them with them on your social media accounts. If other people seem to like you, most women will presume you're okay to get out with.

Women Prefer Males Who Are Superior To Them

Numerous studies have shown that women are unlikely to marry men with lower incomes, less education, or who belong to a lower socioeconomic class than they do. This is evidence of female hypergamy.

It goes deeper than this, at least in my experience as a relationship counselor. A woman's appeal will decrease if a modern man acts in a way that suggests he views her as superior.

Women will never date simpletons because of this. A lady can only treat you like a fan when you treat her like a celebrity. When you simp for your crush, she might express gratitude but won't respect you. Women know that a quality man must be courted to receive their attention.

Women Will Act Rude To Test If A Guy Is The Real Deal

Women desire a man who exudes confidence and masculinity. The issue is that they can't tell immediately if you possess these traits.

If they're amenable to anything you say, you can fool them for a while. This is why a woman often comes off as a little careless while speaking to potential romantic partners. Mind you, not that she's a total bitch. She usually does this to determine whether you are the real deal.

She will be more drawn to you if you maintain your composure and avoid reacting to her.

Women Want A Man They Can Rely On, But Only If He Looks Good

Even though an alpha male may produce champion offspring, if the mother is abandoned, that does no good, not for the kids or her.

Therefore, a lady must look for the most attractive companion who will also be devoted to her. She needs allegiance and attraction.

Sadly, it isn't easy to find a man with both traits. Because they have more options, the most handsome men are also the ones that stray the most.

In light of the current "hook-up culture," this is increasingly obvious to women. On dating apps, they are all pursuing the same men, having sex, and then being dumped. Many women waste their finest years continually repeating this procedure because they are unwilling to lower their standards. They are known as "alpha widows."

There are plenty of women out there who would be willing to date a handsome man who is prepared to commit. The issue is that most men lead with loyalty rather than attracting women. This is a typical 'good guy' mistake that rarely works. Once you've shown that you're an attractive man, women will only desire your romantic gestures.

Building Emotional Connection

You've met a woman who appeals to you. You enjoy being with her, your sexual life has gotten off to a great start, and you want to develop this relationship into something more serious. You want to establish an emotional bond with this woman to accomplish that.

However, it could not be very clear, and you might wonder how to connect emotionally with a woman. You can be afraid of moving the wrong way even though you want to connect with that person so much.

Use these tips to help you genuinely connect with women without frightening them.

One of the most effective, gratifying, and satisfying skills you can learn is how to emotionally connect with a lady (and with people in general). It improves and deepens your connections and allows you to develop yourself.

Read on to learn how to develop this crucial connection with a lady.

Be A Good Communicator

Effective communication is crucial when establishing an emotional connection with a lady. But how do you effectively communicate? You want a decent back-and-forth dialogue when speaking with the woman you are interested in.

While you don't want to monopolize or steer the discussion, you also don't want to appear to be a complete hermit who doesn't respond to her questions.

Your talks should ideally contain an equal exchange of questions and answers.

You want to speak to her without any other interruptions—do not check your phone when it beeps—and pay close attention to her comments.

Rephrase what she said to her to demonstrate that you understood what she said. She might say, "I like to hike on the weekends," for instance. Perhaps you'd say, "It sounds like you enjoy being outside in nature."

This is significantly more effective at teaching you how to establish an emotional connection than simply saying, "Oh, me too."

Express Who You Truly Are

Do you want to know how to relate to real ladies as well? There is an easy solution.

Sincere ladies welcome honesty. It's unlikely for someone who employs all the traditional pick-up lines to develop a strong emotional bond with a lady.

Be genuine. Share your interests with the lady. If you enjoy your job, talk about it. Discuss what you might do to improve the situation if you don't.

If an emotional bond is to develop, it must be between two people who are being completely honest with one another. Be honest and genuine so she can fall in love with you for who you are rather than for some manufactured image you feel you need to project.

Allow your weirdness to fly, even if you don't think it's unusual. She might enjoy your peculiarity!

Permit Her To Open Up And Express Who She Truly Is

You will feel more at ease with one another as your emotional connection grows, which is wonderful. Tell her she may be honest with you and express her hopes, dreams, and anxieties.

You can let her show you her vulnerability and still adore her. For you to connect with her, she doesn't have to be flawlessly coiffed, dressed to the nines, and sporting perfectly coiffed hair. Let her know that as she is, she is perfect.

Kiss And Touch

Continue the non-sexual physical contact. A smart technique to establish an emotional connection with a woman you love is gently kissing her without urging her for more.

Touching her to connect rather than just to indicate "I want to have sex" appeals to women on a profoundly emotional level.

So, as she is cleaning the dishes, kiss her neck. Before you depart for work, give her a firm embrace. If you want to develop a stronger emotional bond with a lady over time, kiss her before bed every single time, even if it is not an act of lovemaking.

Additionally, it answers how to develop intimacy with a lady. Indeed, the important things are always the slow, incremental stages.

Show Your Affection In Many Different Ways

You don't always have to make the "big gestures" to connect emotionally with a woman.

Yes, occasionally giving a woman a rose bouquet, perfume bottle, or a surprise weekend away is appreciated. Smaller, more private displays of affection can strengthen your emotional bond.

Pour her a glass of wine while she begins to make dinner. While you're watching TV, propose to massage her back. Put a sweet note in her bag as she prepares for a work trip. All of these affectionate expressions might strengthen your emotional bond.

Express Your Admiration For Her

This one is quite simple. You can take some actions: Inform her of your pride in her when she overcomes a personal or professional hurdle. Let her see the awe you feel when you gaze upon her. Tell others about her successes when you are out with friends. On Mother's Day, thank her mother for raising such a wonderful daughter. This is also effective if you're new to dating and wondering how to get along with a girl you like.

Furthermore, return to the good old days and sincerely compliment your girlfriend if things have gotten stale recently and you're wondering how to reconnect with her. The spark will undoubtedly return, and she will grin with joy.

Support Them As They Face Health Issues

Going through a health scare together will strengthen your emotional bond more than anything else. If she is facing a health challenge, be there for her. Ask her how you can help. Take her if she needs to visit the hospital for testing. If possible, be there to support her during the testing process.

Let her know she can rely on you to support her as a team as you navigate these tense situations.

Maximize The Time You Have Together

How can you make a girl feel something for you? We are all emotional beings; spending quality time with your partner can help strengthen and develop your emotional bond.

It will be tough to forge an emotional bond if you get into routines like binge-watching the newest Netflix series on the weekends, abusing alcohol, or sleeping all day.

This is a result of your lack of significant engagement. While occasionally watching television or playing video games is acceptable, avoid making these activities a habit. You'll pass up the opportunity to forge an intense emotional bond with a lady and some of the most romantic moments you may share with your lover.

Free Goodwill

Greetings, aspiring Alpha Male,

Before we start the chapter about how to become irresistible, I want to acknowledge your willingness to understand and succeed in dating and relationships before we go into the details of this next chapter. You've made a tremendous advancement toward realizing your potential and developing deep relationships with women.

I now invite you to share your experiences and learnings with others who are zealous about realizing their Alpha Male potential. Your experiences and discovered information might serve as an example for guys who want to develop their seductiveness, self-confidence, and irresistibility to women.

By leaving an honest review of this book, you help other men trying to discover their inner Alpha Male. Your words can inspire and instruct others, pointing them toward developing compelling confidence and irresistible charm.

Consider for a moment the changes you have through as a result of this book. Tell us about the dating hacks, strategies, and mentality changes that most resonate with you. Your review has the potential to inspire others to develop and become the best versions of themselves in their love endeavors.

Let's work together to create a community of men committed to becoming exceptional Alpha Males.

This is as easy as writing a review—a gesture that takes only a few seconds but has a big impact.

Your review can serve as a springboard for one's development and empowerment while encouraging a sense of unity among people trying to establish enduring bonds and satisfying connections.

I send you my best wishes for unshakeable resolve, allure, and remarkable success as you pursue your goal of becoming the Alpha Male you were meant to be!

With gratitude,

Eric Holt

4
Becoming Irresistible

Being a red-blooded male, you find nothing more alluring than a stunning woman's scorching appearance.

But wait a moment. Do not believe that ladies also desire that. Many of the males I know that resemble Brad Pitt are still unable to attract women.

Women can be extremely fussy in romantic relationships, which is not surprising. They are very clear about the qualities they seek in a man, so you might be in trouble if you fall short on even one of these.

I've compiled a list of qualities women value in a man to help you. If you follow this advice, ladies will immediately find you more appealing.

The Alpha Man's Guide To Flirting

Being an "alpha male" refers to a man's dominance, self-confidence, and strength. It entails understanding what you want and getting it. Alpha males are often loved and imitated because they appear to get what they desire constantly. There are a few things you need to do — and avoid — if you respect the alpha male mindset and want to apply it to your personal life to flirt with a girl "the alpha way."

How to Approach Women Confidently

- **Move Like A Dominant Male -** Avoid stumbling onto the girl's friend group before approaching her and clumsily attempting to converse. An alpha male approaches the girl he wants to flirt with directly, confidently, and purposefully. Walk more deliberately and slowly to project control. As lame as it sounds, do not hesitate to practice your walk in your home. Look for a location with mirrors so you can look at yourself. Don't be ashamed to practice a little; sometimes, people have unnoticeable twitches of nervousness.

- **Establish Eye Contact -** It can be daunting to stare directly into a girl's eyes when chatting with her, especially if she is quite attractive. But if you avert your sight, it implies that you think she is beyond your reach. Most women won't be enticed to flirt with a man who has already instinctively expressed his feelings of unworthiness. Make eye contact as you begin a conversation and identify yourself. This does not imply that you should stare at her; doing so can be unsettling. It's acceptable to look away periodically.

- **Say "Hello" With A Firm, Confident Voice -** Wait until there is a little lull in the conversation if she is talking before saying something like, "I'm sorry to interrupt, but I had to come to say hello." It's a positive sign if she seems a little surprised. You've already clarified to her that you're self-confident and won't hold back when going after what you want. To demonstrate your maturity, extend your hand for a handshake. Be sure to clasp her hand firmly enough for her to understand that you feel confident in your interaction.

- **Don't Use Pick-Up Lines** - Don't act like you're reading a flirting textbook to chat with her; women are drawn to sincerity. Confidently explain to her why you approached her. Anything goes, from "I saw you from across the room, and I had to come to say hi to someone so gorgeous" to "I wanted to introduce myself to someone with such a lovely smile."Make sure you have another sensible opening prepared if you don't want to start with a compliment out of concern that it will seem corny. If you have friends in common, you can say, "You're friends with ___, right?" I had to come to say hi because I recognized you. A simple statement like, "I noticed you're eating _____, isn't it excellent?" might be used to start a conversation. You can prevent awkward silences by planning to say in advance.

Dialogue And Flirting

- **Ask Her Questions** - You may steer the conversation this way. Controlling a conversation does not include talking over her, cutting her off, or coming out as a snob. It implies that you are directing the discussion. Asking her personal questions will help you steer the discussion and demonstrate your interest in finding out more about her. Ask her standard opening questions rather than anything intense or private.You can enquire about her relationship with the host at a party. Ask her basic questions about herself while you're out and about, such as her name, what she does, where she's from, and similar topics. After learning more about her, you can ask her more specific, in-depth questions.

- **Use Fewer Words** - Don't jump into lengthy stories or monologues about your life; only discuss yourself when suitable. Let her talk more about herself than you do, and only bring up personal topics when she brings them up or when you want to emphasize a trait you share. The more you listen intently to her and the more she can communicate about herself, the better.

- **Keep Your Tone Upbeat And Pleasant** - Males in the alpha position never whine and feel sorry for themselves. Avoid being a "Debbie Downer" when talking to the female you're interested in because people make their realities. Use your sense of humor if you have one! A highly effective flirting tactic is making a girl laugh. Don't whine because you want her to identify you with happiness, laughter, and p leasure.If she says anything unfavorable, agree with her assessment while casting it more favorably. If she mentions the bad weather, you can respond by saying, "It's not great, but at least we can suffer through it together."

- **Offer Sincere Praise** - Don't try to win her over by showering her with compliments. Mention the appealing traits you find in her. Alpha males don't say things they don't truly mean since they are confident in themselves. This will not only demonstrate your sincerity to her, but it will also increase the value of your kind compliments.If she discusses her work, you could remark, "It sounds like you're very intelligent to manage all of that." If you want to make her laugh with a joke, you may say, "You have a unique chuckle. I enjoy it. Simply telling her she's attractive won't make you appear an alpha male.

- **Make A Joke** - Do not hesitate to tease her lightly. Alpha males exude confidence and aren't afraid to be sincere. Avoid saying anything that would truly offend her, but instead, make her laugh by pointing out her silly behavior. Acting like you've known a woman for ages is a wonderful way to start a playful back-and-forth with her. You can add something like, "Oh [say her name], you've always been so funny/clumsy/stubborn/observant/nerdy." if she begins to talk a little about herself. By making her laugh and feel at ease, you can attract her.

- **Let The Discussion Develop Naturally** - Don't approach a female with the sole intention of getting a date. Instead, set out to engage in a wonderful, flirtatious conversation. In contrast to flirting, which is far more lighthearted, enjoyable, and noncommittal, "picking them up" is usually obvious to women. Let the discussion go naturally, and only make an approach if it feels right.

- **Term Out The Discussion** - Once you've talked for a while, respectfully stop the discussion. Ask her for a date or get her number if everything goes well. Inform her that you enjoyed meeting and speaking with her if you know you will see her again. You've reaffirmed your alpha-ness by concluding the conversation on your terms. During a gap in the conversation, you can remark, "It's been nice chatting with you, and I will [give you a call/see you later/whatever]." Do not worry or fret if things don't go well or she doesn't appear interested. It doesn't matter that sometimes even alpha males get rejected. Keep going because this is the secret to being an alpha: you don't need anyone else to validate you. Nothing to fear from rejection.

Having A Look Of An Alpha

- **Look Fantastic** - This does not imply that you must immediately lose weight, shave off your favorite beard, or spend much money on new clothing. Determine your definition of "great" and embody it. Do it if it will help you stay active and get fitter. Do your hair a quick brush if that's all it takes. Feeling your best is key to being an alpha and flirting like one. Clean up whatever you believe will make you appear better, groom yourself as you prefer, and always remember to be the best version of yourself, whatever that means to you, whenever you meet a female. There are alpha males with the physique of Zac Efron, complete with massive muscles and impeccable attire. Like Bill Clinton, other alpha males find strength in their intelligence and self-confidence. Outward appearance has less to do with being an alpha male than thinking.

- **Keep Up Good Hygiene** - While personal choices like your hairdo and clothing are your own, maintaining excellent hygiene is essential. You can't be filthy or unpleasant to be around if you want the best chance of getting girls. Maintain clean skin and hair, take frequent showers, and keep your breath smelling good. While keeping poor hygiene habits can make it easy to flirt, cleanliness will undoubtedly improve your chances.

- **Understand The Difference Between Cocky And Alpha** - Having a confident, "alpha" demeanor can occasionally be mistaken for being cocky. An alpha is self-confident, flexible, and doesn't need to control the conversation or constantly be the focus of attention. They understand that they are only human, just like everyone else, and that they occasionally make mistakes. Contrarily, a cocky person is arrogant (his self-esteem is built primarily on wealth, privilege, and external circumstances), will talk over other people, be ruthless in their pursuit of success, and will not acknowledge their mistakes or offer an apology. A fully self-confident individual can take criticism in stride, let someone else take center stage, and own up to mistakes (without overcompensating).

- **Be A Confident Person** - Don't be scared to take up space while maintaining a straight posture. Alpha males won't be slumped and twitching their hands or clothing nervously. Breathe deeply and tell yourself that you are the most attractive man there. If you're standing, have a wide posture and keep your arms at your sides. Regardless of your feelings, concentrate on projecting an air of ease, confidence, and dominance. To look like an alpha male is similar to working out a new muscle. The more times you do it, the easier it gets. You'll eventually begin to experience what it's like to be an alpha male.

Seduction Techniques That Drive Women Wild

Learning to seduce a girl will require effort and knowledge of the female psyche. However, we have confidence in you and know you can succeed.

Although you might believe it's a simple technique, you must approach this assignment with a sharp mind to succeed.

Learn about these suggestions, implement them, and determine which is effective. Guys, it's time to get to work. Use this manual to arouse her sexual desire for you.

Recognize That Every Girl Is Unique

You won't be able to approach each girl in the same way. Why? You need to understand that not all girls are created equal.

Once you understand it, you'll speak to each girl differently rather than treat them equally. Surely not all men are the same? And women are not either.

Pay Attention To Seducing Her Mind First

Women are thought and feeling creatures. It's closely related to their mental health when they experience an orgasm. So, sex is not just physical for girls; it is also psychological.

Similar rules apply to seduction. You must engage a girl's thoughts to know how to seduce her; sending a sexy picture won't cut it. Talk about something captivating and encourage her to engage her imagination by using visual language.

Girls Enjoy Laughing

There is one thing that the majority of females desire in a partner: laughter. But that makes logical, right?

However, be careful not to overdo it; her laughter must be genuine. It's also possible that your sense of humor doesn't align with hers, and that's fine. Trust us; there will be another girl who will enjoy your jokes.

Avoid Being Overt In Your Attempts To Seduce Her

Everyone wants to remain unaware of their seduction. It makes it less enjoyable for you both. Consider this a test for both you and her.

What happens if you tell her, "I'm going to seduce you," then? Not much. Maintain some mystery while taking in the experience.

Refrain From Acting Immediately

Don't kiss her, even if we know you want to. Nothing works better to create sexual tension than depriving her of what she desires. The intention is to make her angry that you didn't approach her.

So, move slowly because some annoyance is healthy.

Display Your Inherent Confidence

If you enter a room looking insecure, you will never succeed in learning how to seduce a girl. You must project an air of ownership. The problem is that you have to feel it genuinely.

Fake it till you make it if you lack confidence. It is the only option. But keep in mind that exaggerating your confidence might potentially backfire. Be yourself and have faith in yourself.

Focus On Her Face Instead Of Her Boobs

This is the most significant thing you shouldn't do. Keep an eye out. Don't treat her like a set of boobs; we know you want to glance down, but you want to charm her.

Keep your eyes open, participate in the discussion, and display intellectual interest. Show some decency!

Figure Out Her Preferences

You should consider her preferences. She wants a relationship, not just a one-night stand, right? Observe her desires.

Now, you don't have to approach her directly; instead, use indirect questions to try and ascertain her interests. This way, you are aware of how to approach her.

Avoid Giving The Impression That You Want To Sleep With Her

If you're speaking with her, you want to take things further. We are aware of that. You do, also. That is common knowledge. This does not, however, imply that you treat her like a piece of meat.

Girls can distinguish between a man genuinely interested in them and one wanting to put her to bed. She might be into it if she likes the guy, but she doesn't think you misled her.

She most likely was aware of your plans from the beginning. And at this point, she would question if she should keep talking to you.

Avoid Using Too Many Cliched Pick-Up Lines

Do not use them if you are not required to. Not knowing what to say to a female, then? Simply introduce yourself to her.

She will chat with you if she likes you. It's lame and dries out the pants to use some "did you fall from heaven" phrase. Believe us.

Establish A Softly Romantic Ambiance

You are in control of creating a romantic mood between you no matter where you are, whether it's a club or a cafe. Therefore, You should sit near her, look her in the eye, smile, and chuckle to show interest.

Make her feel loved and appreciated. You want to be subtle and romantic, so don't go overboard.

Only Touch Her In Certain Places

Avoid getting too close to her, or you'll appear too aggressive. You should touch her, but just in areas that aren't too sexual or too passive.

You can, for example, touch her lower back. But avoid touching her behind! You're more likely to receive a smack than a token of appreciation. You are allowed to touch her knee, arms, and shoulders.

But be sure to watch her closely; stop if she flinches, retreats, or otherwise seems uneasy.

Don't Ask Your Friends For Help

Seriously, you're no longer a child. Initially, you can use a wingman, but you should try to approach a woman on your own.

You know you've made it when you can approach a woman without the help of a friend to serve as your wingman. Although friends might be useful, going it alone presents the most challenge.

Always Stay True To Who You Are

You must be true to who you are, which is very important. Many men have attempted to seduce women but failed because they are trying to pass for someone else.

Why try to act differently? We know that some guys appear to attract women consistently, but it is just because of who they are. Seduction shouldn't change who you are; rather, it should highlight your positive traits.

Go Slowly

Keep in mind that you are not competing when it comes to seduction. The opposite outcome will occur if a woman feels pushed or under pressure. She must always feel valued, taken care of, and at ease.

You're not competing for a medal here, so slow down!

Dress For Success

If you look good, you make an impression on her and feel better about yourself. Dress smartly, avoid wearing anything too bright or flashy, and choose an appropriate outfit.

You want to project an air of confidence while maintaining a dapper appearance. The poor girl will go away if you wear too much color.

If you haven't taken the time to shower, style your hair, and apply a little cologne before you leave the house, she won't be very impressed with your clothes, no matter how great it is.

Listen To Her

Being confident and taking over the conversation are two different things. The conversation must be two-way if you want her to feel at ease and as though she's getting to know you better.

Show her that you are paying attention by paying attention to what she has to say.

Be Sure Not To Ask Too Many Questions

Make sure you grill her with questions as well. Instead of just getting her into the bedroom, this demonstrates to her that you are interested in her and genuinely want to get to know her as a person.

A woman is more likely to desire to advance a situation if she feels safe and comfortable doing so. But refrain from interrogating her in an interview-style manner. That will produce the exact opposite result.

Pay Attention To What She Needs

Make sure you fill her wine glass if it's empty. Offer her your jacket if she appears to be cold. It's all about paying attention to the minor details here and there.

She will also consider you incredibly romantic and lovely and the type of guy who knows how to treat a lady well.

Compliment Her

Make sure she is aware of your admiration for her beauty. Timing is everything when complimenting a woman. Be sure to wait for a pause in the conversation or retain her attention and say, "Sorry, I just can't get over how pretty you are."

The secret to compliments is to ensure they are not overpowering but explicit enough for her to understand that you are truly drawn to her.

Slightly Intrude On Her Personal Space

If you want to make a move, move your chair closer to hers while you're having dinner or out for drinks, or brush her hand over the table or her leg below it - but, as we said before, pay attention to how she responds.

You might advise taking her for a walk while holding her hand or dancing where you can touch her. If you're going on a date at home, position yourself closer to her after you're more relaxed on your sofa.

Always Remember Not To Push Things!

Even if you follow all the necessary steps, there are situations when the chemistry just isn't there. Avoid trying to force anything if she isn't responding well. Accept that you can't win them all, and cut your losses!

5
Dating Strategies For Alpha Men

The dating scene is a disgrace nowadays. Even if "it didn't work" and the evening didn't turn out how you had hoped, going on a date can still be one of the most enjoyable experiences you'll ever have. I'm not exaggerating. Instead, dating resembles a job interview where the employer (I'll let you guess who's boss in the setting) somehow suffers. I'd like to provide you with some advice and a healthy dating strategy in this chapter so that you'll meet many ladies and, more importantly, have a great time.

Navigating The Dating Scene With Confidence

The dating environment can be thrilling and overwhelming for those just starting. It isn't easy to know where to start when there are many methods to meet possible partners, from dating apps to gatherings. But worry not—anyone can succeed in dating with a little self-awareness, confidence, and sincerity. In this chapter, we'll discuss some advice for finding love, remaining loyal to yourself, and having fun while doing it. So, let's get ready to embrace the great dating world and dive right in!

Get To Know Yourself

Knowing yourself is the first step to navigating the dating world. This entails giving your beliefs, goals, and boundaries some thought. Finding a partner who is the right match for you requires that you be aware of your needs and preferences.

Spend some time considering who you are and what that means to you. This can entail getting advice from friends, joining a group of supporters, or even going to therapy. Whatever you do, wait until you're confident before entering a relationship.

Be Real With Yourself

Finding a companion who is a good match for you requires being real. It's unlikely that pretending to be someone you're not to impress your date would result in a happy and healthy relationship. Be authentic and certain that the appropriate person will value and adore you for who you are.

Use Dating Apps

Finding love is now much easier, thanks to dating apps. You can contact people from all over the world with just a swipe or tap. But they can also be frustrating and stressful.

Being deliberate and picky is essential for success with dating apps. Spend time making a profile that truly captures your personality and dating preferences. Make use of recent, quality photographs and state your aims clearly.

Before committing to a face-to-face meeting, take the time to get to know possible matches when you start conversing with them. Ask questions, reveal your hobbies, and determine whether there is a connection using the messaging section of the app.

Have Fun And Stay Secure

While dating should be thrilling and engaging, putting your safety first is crucial. This entails exercising caution when approaching strangers and keeping yourself safe.

For your first date, meet in a public location and let a friend or relative know where you'll be and who you'll be with. Trust your gut feelings, and don't be afraid to say "no" or "go" if something doesn't feel right.

In any relationship, communication is essential, so be open and sincere with your partner. Discuss your limits, aspirations, and expectations with others while paying attention to theirs. Most essential, enjoy meeting new people and having fun while doing so.

Finally, navigating the dating world can be fun and fulfilling, but putting your needs and safety first is crucial. You can find a mate that loves and accepts you for who you are by being true to yourself and real and taking precautions to protect yourself. Who knows, you might even stumble upon the love of your life.

The Art Of Making A Powerful First Impression

You'll never have another chance to make a good first impression! Although it's cliche, it's true. A woman will remember your first impression for the duration of her relationship. I assume that the phenomenon of falling in love at first sight, has a lot to do with the fact that research suggests that the seeds of love are often planted during a first impression.

I'm sure you've heard about the importance of first impressions. When you first meet a lady, you tend to pay close attention to everything she does and says. You may even take note of little facts that may help you build an opinion of her. You need to make a strong first impression and give ladies that "love at first sight" feeling to attract them quickly. Here are a few strategies for maximizing your first impression.

Quickly Initiate The Action

If you spot a woman and catch her attention, move quickly to initiate contact. She will react less instinctively and more overthink the situation the longer you wait to approach her.

For instance, if you make eye contact with a woman at a bar who notices you, she will get interested. She will still be aroused if you approach her right away, but if you wait too long, she may begin to create an impression about you that may be unfavorable. In other words, you want to get involved and say and do things that will give her the first image you want her to have of you rather than leaving it up to her imagination.

Maintain A Close Gaze

Yes, making eye contact with a woman indicates your interest in her, but it also accomplishes another task. The 'love at first sight' engine is cranked up, and a strong attraction is produced!

It's easy to understand why. When two people are in love, they look into each other's eyes. They stare for extended periods as their love grows. It fosters a powerful sense of connection and affection. Even if you don't have a close relationship with a lady, you can simulate that emotion by giving her a loving glance.

This requires you to look a woman in the eyes more often than usual. Hold your gaze for at least 70%, whether speaking to her or just trying to capture her attention. This will increase the eye contact without becoming excessive and rekindle her sentiments of love. She won't understand why she feels such a strong bond with you, but she will.

Wear A Red Item

Red is an attention-grabbing hue. It is utilized in sirens, stops lights, stop signs, fire engines, etc. because of this, women take notice of this color. Red can make people feel scared or angry, but it can also make them feel passionate in the appropriate situation. Think of a red dress or a woman's red lipstick.

Wearing red lipstick won't help you make a good first impression or draw attention from ladies. It'll just not work. But you can spice up your ensemble with some crimson. Put on something red, such as a hat, tie, or dress shirt. You only need to match the color of your red with a tiny bit of passion in your personality for women to notice it! The first impression is crucial in the end. Create sensations of attraction that resemble the sensation of falling in love at first sight rather than just making a nice first impression.

Limit Your Hand Gestures

If you want to convey the message of confidence, control, and focus, don't run up to a woman flapping your hands and twitching your body like you have too much energy. This type of movement communicates that you don't feel at ease in your skin. Women won't feel comfortable with you, too.

You want to maintain control over your body and project a calm demeanor. Gestures should be used, but only when necessary. Doing this will demonstrate that you are in charge and a calm, confident person to be around.

Keep A Swaggering Stance

Approaching a woman hunched over, your arms folded, and your gaze on the ground is not advised. No matter how well you communicate with her, this body language will reflect a lack of confidence or a bad attitude. In either case, it's not a favorable attitude.

Keep your head up, pull your shoulders back, and carry yourself with pride to convey that you are a man deserving of respect and adoration. A woman will want to meet you again if you have a posture like that when making a first impression.

Be Upbeat But Not Overly So

Getting a positive first impression from a negative guy who moans about everything is hard. Women who encounter such kind of guy will start counting down the seconds until they can leave, and they will never look back. Women will expect your best behavior, and having a nasty attitude shouldn't be your best conduct while making a first impression.

Your cheerful attitude will always improve a woman's perception of you. Just be careful not to overdo it. When you sing about the sun and lollipops, you could be a little insane. Simply communicate that you are pleased and that you love life.

Discuss Pertinent Issues

You shouldn't discuss topics you regularly discuss with friends during a first impression. Avoid talking about anything personal. When you talk about how frustrated you are right now, the woman you are speaking to cannot understand what you are truly trying to express since she is unaware of your beliefs and values.

Discuss your surroundings. Talk about the similarities you two share. Discuss the individual seated next to you. Keep the talk on the topic and avoid too much personal stuff.

Pay Attention To Her Nonverbal Cues

Watch her body language to see what kind of impression you are creating on her. You can give a terrible first impression if she backs away from you, folds her arms, or raises her eyebrows. You should change your voice, subject matter, or body language in such cases.

However, suppose she is grinning, appearing at ease, and maintaining eye contact with you. In that case, you can assume you are creating a positive first impression and continue your actions.

Ask Questions

You are almost certainly talking about yourself, your views, or your beliefs when you are not asking questions. You risk coming across as selfish if you talk too much about yourself. Selfishness is a major turnoff when making a first impression.

Try to engage in conversation to seem interested in her. She will perceive you as someone who genuinely cares about her and what she has to say if you give her more opportunities to express herself or voice her thoughts and beliefs. If you can demonstrate your concern for them, women (and other people) will always want to see you again.

Be Sincere

You might need to be a little more formal in your communication during a first impression, but you still need to be genuine. If you want to impress a woman, avoid agreeing to something you disagree with.

Don't speak to her in a way that contrasts with how you often speak just to impress her. If you uphold your ideals and ideas and remain loyal to who you are, you will come across better. (Just be careful not to impose your opinions on others, or they may perceive you as intrusive.)

Display Good Manners

Nobody enjoys rude people. She will have a negative impression of you and mark you as someone she does not want to see again if you are impolite, arrogant, or careless.

Be sure to be considerate and pay attention to her feelings as well as the feelings of those around you. They will see that you care about others and have emotional intelligence if you are nice.

Maintain Good Hygiene

This may sound apparent, but there are instances when we can leave the house without considering how we look, leading to several poor first impressions. People quickly form opinions based on looks, so even if you come across as well-mannered, intelligent, and humorous at first, they will still base most of their judgment on how you dress and look.

No matter what, always leave your house dressed to impress to give the finest first impression wherever you go, regardless of whether you think you won't run into a woman.

Keep The Conversation Going

A woman won't want to meet with you again if you have nothing to say and there are a lot of awkward silences in your chat. This is because you will likely produce an awful first impression. That is not what you want to happen! You must therefore maintain a flow in your conversation.

It's not difficult to come up with conversation starters. All you have to do is pay attention to the woman speaking to you and note any odd remarks they make. They will only bring up things they enjoy, consider, or are aware of. A reference to a person, location, or event is possible.

For instance, if she says that the rain will be good for the gardens while it is raining outside, she probably has some form of attraction to gardens. When you run out of topics to discuss, bring up her comment about gardens; she'll undoubtedly have much to say.

Make the most of your initial impression by using the 11 tips above. Never discount the power of a first impression. Women may want to see you again if you leave a good impression. Furthermore, if you don't leave a favorable impression, it may be impossible to do so again.

6
Balancing Inner And Outer Strength

Without thinking, what immediately springs to mind when you think about self-care? Do you instantly picture a woman treating herself to a bubble bath? Or a candle-lit chamber where she reads Fifty Shades of Grey while sipping wine? Self-care is a series of rituals, routines, or practices (they can be as basic as you like) that help people recharge, refocus, and balance their personal pleasure and well-being. Self-care involves more than just treating oneself; it also requires effort and time. And males should unquestionably put it into practice as well.

What Exactly Is Self-Care, And Why Do Men Need It?

Self-care is nothing more than making time for oneself. You set aside a certain time during the day, or even once a week, to put your stressors on hold to enhance your mental health. Because of the absolute instability of recent years, attention to and emphasis on mental health have increased. Self-care should be prioritized since, during the pandemic, more than one in three persons in the United States reported having symptoms of anxiety or depression.

Men are behind the times and might not even know where to start with self-care because it has historically been seen (and advertised) as something that women do more often than men. But why even bother making time for self-care for men? We must therefore maintain our physical, mental, and emotional well-being, just like women.

There is no "one-size-fits-all" self-care approach because it is a deeply individualized activity. The beauty is that you may define self-care as whatever you like as long as it keeps you physically and psychologically healthy.

Nurturing The Body, Mind, And Soul

What is the most effective method for healing our ailments? Your physician prescribed you a medication to balance your serotonin levels. Having a couple of drinks after work to decompress? Or perhaps you overate to ease your depressive thoughts? Simple, fast remedies that temporarily alleviate the symptoms never result in long-lasting relief.

Over the years, I've tried several methods to quell my fearful thoughts. In the past, I would choose the quick and simple route. At first, I didn't realize they added to my worries. I eventually realized that something had to change.

Today, I have a variety of tried-and-true techniques that revolve around nature. We have internal and exterior treatments for the mind, body, and soul. I've been learning about and experimenting with these natural cures for years.

I provide these in the hope that they would enable anyone to be patient, willing, and able to fully submit to Mother Nature's curative forces. The majority of them are open to everyone and free. All you have to do is have faith.

Take A Breath

How often do we take the opportunity to tune out the outside world and concentrate on what's happening inside? Turn off the screen and put the phone down. Switch on and listen for a while. Pay notice to how the air is causing your lunges to expand, your chest to rise, and your heart to beat higher. Release and let go of everything as you exhale. Make sure to breathe into your belly while maintaining regulated, deep breathing.

Meditate

After practicing breath control, we can use meditation to go even further into our hearts and thoughts. Now that science has acknowledged the advantages of extended time alone, it has adapted to old traditions. Meditation can be practiced in any method. To help you reach nirvana, utilize incense, breathing exercises, and music. Simply allow your ideas to come and go, surrender, and smile. Creating a mantra of uplifting affirmations to repeat repeatedly will help you realign your thoughts with your authentic, unadulterated self.

Spend Time Outside

This world, which is a living, breathing, and incredibly self-nurturing place, is where we were created. We spend 90%

BALANCING INNER AND OUTER STRENGTH

of our time inside on average. We were meant to live more wild lives; thus, this is not good for our bodily, spiritual, or emotional health. Okay, so I'm not advocating that we all migrate into the woods (would anyone like to? No, just me) and collect dandelion leaves and go rabbit hunting, but escaping the stresses of modern life by strolling amid the trees and birds is calming to the soul. We re-establish our connection to our roots by initiating Mother Nature's all-encompassing compassion and healing abilities.

Improve Your Diet

Every component of our beings receives messages from the meals we eat. Focus on consuming full, raw, natural foods in your diet. Avoid processed foods, especially those that include refined sugars, and use alcohol and caffeine in moderation. Alcohol is a poison that makes both body and mind feel lethargic. It's acceptable in moderation now and again, but abusing it regularly may harm your physical, emotional, and spiritual well-being. I have once more cut out meat, but this time I mean it. If you do, ensure it's the best possible quality and isn't consumed frequently.

Moving More

Your body was created to move. Injuries and illnesses can result from idleness. Make it a habit of standing up often if you sit in a chair for long periods. Do a few bodyweight squats while moving around and stretching your spine. Many people's back, and hip problems are caused by prolonged sitting.

Additionally, discover a practice that speaks to you deeply on every level of your existence. It won't ever feel like work. It will always be advantageous.

Put Sleep First

The miracle drug, and rightfully so. We can access this exquisitely created interior dream world for mind and body healing. Make it a habit to sleep more than 7 hours every night. Leave the technology behind and your issues behind. As they said, it's a good idea to sleep on them.

Herbal Infusions And Teas

Nothing compares to a nice old brew. Through the decades, numerous societies have relied on tea, infusions, and diverse concoctions to treat illnesses. A morning cup of green tea can be calming because of its delicate flavor. A cup of ginger and lemon tea can energize and warm the spirit in the chilly winter. After a meal, a cup of mint tea can help with digestion. The world of plants is full of healing magic that can be discovered.

Supplementation

Supplementing your diet with minerals and vitamins may be helpful once you've followed the previous remedies. Generally speaking, a diet high in various fruits and vegetables should be sufficient to meet most people's needs. The only exceptions are persons engaging in intense physical activity or those with a recognized vitamin shortage.

Managing Stress And Overcoming Burnout

BALANCING INNER AND OUTER STRENGTH

According to research, a significant portion of Americans experience work-related stress, which is rising. A poll of more than 2,000 full-time U.S. employees aged 18 to 79 found that more than half of workers experience stress for at least 60% of the workweek.

Work stress has numerous negative effects on health, ranging from relatively minor ones like an increase in colds and flu to potentially dangerous ones like heart disease and metabolic syndrome.

Finding a career with low stress is difficult, if not impossible, despite workplace stress is common. Adopting efficient coping mechanisms to lessen stress on your existing employees is a more practical course of action. By maintaining a positive morning routine, being clear about your employer's expectations, implementing more effective time management skills, and other tactics described in this section, you can make efforts to control your work stress.

Establish A Pre-Work Ritual

Many individuals arrive at work feeling anxious after rushing to get their children fed and off to school, dodging traffic, dealing with road rage, and downing tea instead of a healthy breakfast. They become more sensitive to workplace stress as a result.

You might be shocked by how much office stress affects you after a challenging morning. If you start the day with planning, a good diet, and a positive mindset, you can find it easier to bear the stress of your job.

Establish Your Day's Expectations Clearly

Uncertain requirements for workers are one issue known to contribute to job burnout. If you don't know what is expected of you or if the demands of your employees keep changing unexpectedly, you may feel a lot of stress.

Talking with your supervisor may be helpful if you often question whether your actions are sufficient. You can spend some time going over expectations and talking about ways to meet them. Both of you will feel less stressed as a result!

Avoid Or Lessen Disagreements With Coworkers

Your emotional and physical health suffers when you are involved in interpersonal strife. It might be challenging to eliminate workplace conflict; therefore, minimizing it wherever possible is a good idea.

Avoid office chit-chat, sharing too many of your political and religious ideas, and avoiding using "colorful" office humor.

Avoid people who don't get along with others if at all possible. If the conflict still finds you, know how to respond effectively.

Plan To Maintain Organization

Planning to keep organized will significantly reduce your stress at work, even if you are naturally disorganized. Being well-organized with your schedule results in less hurrying to get ready in the morning and less hustle to leave at the end of the day.

Maintaining your organization can help you stay productive at work and avoid the drawbacks of clutter.

Establish A Welcoming Work Environment

Physical discomfort, often tied to where you perform most of your daily responsibilities (such as your desk), is another unexpected source of stress at work.

If you sit in an uncomfortable chair for a short period, you might not even notice that you're stressed, but if you spend your entire working day in that chair, you might develop a sore back and become more sensitive to stress.

Even seemingly unimportant things, like workplace noise, might be upsetting and make you feel mildly frustrated. Make every effort to create a quiet, cozy, relaxing workspace.

Chunking Is Preferable To Multitasking

The ability to multitask was formerly hailed as a great method to make the most of one's time and do more daily. However, people quickly realized that their speed and accuracy—not to mention sanity—often decreased if they were performing math while holding a phone to their ear.

Splitting your attention doesn't work well for most individuals because it causes a specific "frazzled" feeling. Try another cognitive method, such as chunking, to keep up with your duties instead of multitasking.

Jog During Lunch

Many people feel the negative impacts of living a sedentary lifestyle. Exercise during your lunch break can help you counteract the negative impacts of work stress on your body and mind.

If your schedule permits, you can take quick breaks to exercise throughout the day. Doing this can relieve stress, improve your attitude, and become in better condition.

Try Your Hardest And Reward Yourself

High achievement can boost your self-esteem and help you flourish at work, but being a perfectionist can harm you (and those around you).

Particularly in hectic, time-constrained work, you might be unable to complete everything flawlessly every time. The easiest way to avoid falling into the perfectionism trap is to aim to do your best and set aside time to acknowledge your achievements. You might discover that your work is much less stressful and your outcomes are better.

Play Music While Driving Home

Numerous advantages of listening to music include stress reduction before, during, and after work. While cooking breakfast, listening to music that inspires you can make you feel more ready to engage with the people in your life when the day starts. Similarly, listening to your favorite music on the way home can help you decompress and feel less anxious after a long day.

Conclusion

Being an alpha male takes some getting used to. This is a learned way of life; nobody is born with it. Pain, discomfort, and difficulty are necessary. But I can assure you that it's worthwhile.

It is impossible to describe the joy you will have after overcoming your "inner nice guy" and creating a life according to your standards. You will approach life with increased vigor, enthusiasm, and energy daily. You'll gain courage, resiliency, and strength. Your life will get better in every way.

However, being an alpha has everything to do with how you see yourself and nothing to do with how other people see you. You won't ever develop into an alpha male if you lack confidence, aren't pursuing your own goals, and aren't seeking guidance from the inside.

Because it's easier, beta males follow the crowd and go with the flow. They are reluctant to upset the status quo because vice has clouded their judgment. An alpha male pursues expansion despite the discomfort. They don't do it to gain something in return; they do it to improve the lives of those around them.

Taking charge of your life and living it fully are essential to becoming an alpha male.

www.ingramcontent.com/pod-product-compliance
Lightning Source LLC
Chambersburg PA
CBHW022120090426
42743CB00008B/939